Exit 32

Rock

Climbing

Guide

By Garth Bruce

Disclaimer

The activities described in this book are potentially dangerous and can result in severe injury or death. The information in this book may be inaccurate and you are fully responsible for all personal injury while approaching or climbing the routes described in this book. Weather conditions in the areas described in this book change continually which can result in dangerous climbing conditions. All the potential hazards are too numerous to list here. If you do not have adequate climbing knowledge and experience, hire a qualified professional instructor. You assume full responsibility and liability when using this guide.

Exit 32 Rock Climbing Guide

Cover Photo
Front Cover - Marcus Hysert on Chronic, 5.13b p. 67
Back Cover - Marcus Hysert off Chronic, 5.13b p. 67
All photos and written material by Garth Bruce unless otherwise stated.

Published and Distributed by
Free Solo Publishing
FreeSoloPublishing@NorthBendRock.com

For my Mother

She has shown me that you never stop growing.

Table of Contents

Exit 32

Introduction

Exit 32 (also known as the Little Si Climbing Area) was one of the first rock climbing locations in the Seattle area. A few adventurous (or as referred to by my mom – mentally challenged) people were scrambling up these crags in the 1950's. It wasn't until the early 1980's that climbing equipment and techniques advanced to the level which allowed the larger vertical and overhanging walls to be exploited by the mentally challenged.

This book shows you many of the most popular walls and routes in the Exit 32 area. This book does not show you how to rock climb nor tell you what equipment you should or shouldn't use. It will also not give you any stock market investment advice or recommend which deodorant works best in the Northwest. If you need information on any of these topics, you should call your mother or ask your local librarian.

If you happen to be new to the area and stop to ask someone about the climbing area in the town of North Bend you're likely to get that deer caught in the headlights look. The main reason is that the climbing area is nestled in a heavily wooded area in the narrow valley between the smaller mountain, Little Si, and the larger Mountain, Si. Only by hiking up the Little Si trail would you notice the large rock walls.

The Exit 32 area is part of the Mount Si Natural Resources Conservation Area which is managed by the State Department of Natural Resources. The climbing area is open for day use only; hence fires and camping are a no-no. The gates in the parking lot are open at 7:00 am and close at 10:00 pm May-August and 9:00 pm September-April. See Appendix C for more rules you'll probably break.

One of the most dangerous aspects of the Exit 32 area isn't at the climbing area, but on the first part of the hiking trail from the parking lot. It's not rock fall hazard nor a steep unstable trail. It's actually much worse. It's processed dog food. For some reason, four legged hikers get extremely excited when they figure out they're going for a hike and let loose on the first section of trail. They seem to empty themselves of excitement quickly because the remainder of the trail is okay.

The climbing area is divided into three sections: British Aisles, Greenland, and New World. British Aisles and Greenland are series of smaller crags that lead up to the larger wall, New World. In general, you will find the easiest climbing (5.5-5.8) at the British Aisles, intermediate level climbs (5.9-5.11) at Greenland, and advanced climbs (5.11-5.14) at New World.

There are several other climbing walls in the Exit 32 area that are not covered in this book. The reasons being they are more remote, trail erosion is a concern, they're completely buried because of overgrowth, or the Washington State Conservation Area has designated it limited public access in order to protect the sensitive areas.

Exit 32 has over a 100 sport routes and over 15 gear routes. Over half the routes range in difficulty from 5.11a to 5.14b and most of the gear routes are between 5.5 and 5.9. In essence, Exit 32 is all about advanced level sport climbing. If you're just getting started in the climbing world then take this book back to the store where you bought it and ask them if they will trade you for a copy of the Exit 38 climbing guide.

If you're new to the area, then first familiarize yourself with it by reading the introduction for each group of walls i.e. British Aisles, Midland, and New World. Pick one of the areas that best match your climbing ability and hiking time requirements. Next, find a computer connected to the internet and surf to http://www.northbendrock.com. It provides the latest information about the climbing area. It also has some very useful panoramic images of the parking areas, trails, and walls which will help you visually familiarize yourself with the areas and make you wish you had a higher speed internet connection.

Although it's very unlikely, you may find some mis takes or needed corrections in this book. If you do find some, please send them to corrections@northbendrock.com. Updates to the book will be published on www.northbendrock.com/bookupdates. If you happen to disagree with some of the route grades, ratings, or beta, send your email to trashcan@northbendrock.com. Just kidding! Send them to corrections@northbendrock.com.

The route difficulty ratings in this book are based on the Yosemite Decimal System (YDS). If you're not familiar with YDS then you should spend some more money and buy an expensive introduction to rock climbing book or enroll in a climbing course. In case you can't afford either of these then here's a quick summary.

Difficulty is broken into 5 classes ranging from easy off-trail hiking (class 1-3), scrambling (class 4), and exposed scrambling (class 5). Class 5 is subdivided into five levels ranging from 5.0 (easiest) to 5.15 (most difficult). In general, Class 5 can be viewed as:

5.0 – 5.5	Easy
5.6 – 5.8	Intermediate
5.9 – 5.10	Hard
5.11 – 5.12	Expert
5.13 – 5.15	Elite

But wait, it gets better. Above 5.10 the ratings are further subdivided by letters ranging from "a" (easier) to "d" (more difficult). So, a route with a difficulty rating of 5.10a would be easier than a route rated at 5.10b.

The chart below shows the range of route difficulty at Exit 32. If you're chart challenged then it says most of the routes are very difficult (Expert – Elite) so your rock skills best be sharp or all you'll be doing is belaying.

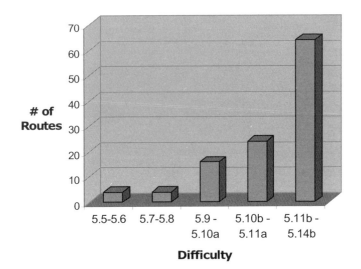

There are three places in the book where you will find strange symbols: on the Wall Maps (topos), the Route Description Tables, and the Route Pictures.

Wall Maps

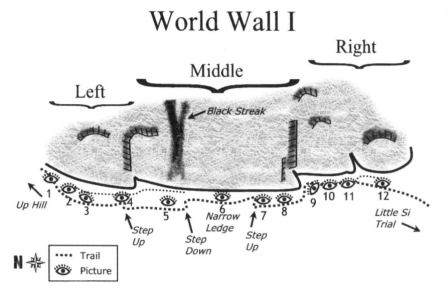

Each climbing wall has a simple topo map. The purpose of the map is to outline how the wall is laid out with respect to the hiking trails, routes, and pictures.

In the example above, World Wall I is separated into three major sections: Left, Middle, and Right. In each of these sections, there are one or more lines dashed lines (---) which indicates the hiking trail or a side trail for a belay ledge. The route picture location icons (👁) and numbers will orient you to where the route picture was taken with respect to the wall.

Note: Some of the climbing wall pictures may seem slightly warped. Don't worry; it's not you that's warped; well, maybe. It's because I used a wide angle camera lens (which curves the image) and then digitally stitched multiple images together, sometimes in a bizarre way.

Route Description Tables

Difficulty	Route	Bolts	Rating	Top Rope	Route Name
5.8	E	8	★★★	No	Human Foot p. 26
5.11b	D	26 (Pro to 9")	★★	✓	Diaper on, Climb on! ❗See Beta p. 334

Difficulty: Yosemite Decimal System number. An "estimate" of the effort needed to reach the top and is usually determined by the person who installed the route.

Route: Letters A-Z. Used to identify the specific route in the picture. Listed in ascending order from left to right.

Bolts: Number from 1-15. Number of bolts on the route, not including anchor. If additional protection (Pro) is required, it is listed in parenthesis with the largest piece needed.

Rating: 1 to 4 stars. Route fun factor; 4 stars given to the best routes.

★★★★	Do whatever it takes to get on the route (bribe someone, wait in line for days, climb it at night …)
★★★	A good, rewarding route that will enrich your life
★★	Imagine it's a 4-star route
★	Probably a nice route… if you could find it under the moss

Top Rope: Checkmark (✓) or No. Checkmark means you can safely hike to the top of the routes and run a rope through the chains with minimal risk to you and other climbers below.

Route Name: The name given by the person who created the route. A bold explanation point (❗) at the beginning of the route name means there is potential danger and you should read the beta notes in the route index on the listed page before climbing.

Route Pictures

Every route listed in this book has an associated picture. Most of the pictures will show two or more routes. Because of the lens distortion, time of day, condition of the rock, condition of the photographer and so forth, the picture may look slightly different from what you see.

Below is a typical picture which has three symbols:

 : Yosemite Decimal System (YDS) route rating number followed by a letter to identify the route.

 : Anchors at the top of the route, usually two sections of chain.

 : Approximate route path you might follow.

 : The picture and page number on the topo reference map, e.g. picture number "6" on page number "28".

Appendix A, p. 80, lists the climbing routes sorted by difficulty and quality (star) rating. The table also contains the sometimes important, and sometimes worthless, but always entertaining beta descriptions. The name following the beta is the person who provided the beta.

Some of the route listings will have an explanation point (**!**) which means there is potential danger. Make sure you read the beta description in the route listing table. It will tell you what the potential risk is and how to mitigate it.

FA: stands for "First Ascent." This means the first person who successfully redpointed the route which is usually the one who created it. If two or more people are listed, then the rules are as follows:

- Second Person: Did most of the work to create the route (carried all the equipment, cleaned the route, etc.) but can't afford a drill.

- Third Person: Did little to no work but bought beer afterward.

- Fourth, Fifth, Sixth…: Friends to whom the creator is indebted for money, bolt and hanger donations, gas, food, lodging, etc.

Here's an example of a typical route entry in the route listings table in Appendix A:

Difficulty	Route Name	Rating	Area	Beta
5.11b	Monkey Madness p. 48	★★	Woods	Start up the Monkey bar like holds to a lean face and then finish on more Monkey bars. FA: John Heiman

> *If you don't know where you're going, you'll end up somewhere else.*
>
> *- Yogi Bera*

There are eight primary climbing walls in the Exit 32 area. They are all part of the same large ridge of rock that runs along the eastern side of the Little Si Mountain. As you continue north up the trail the walls grow larger and culminate into a major rock face.

The lower walls (British Aisles and Greenland) are only a 100 meters apart and could be considered one section but, given there is a trail to each (and I needed to add pages so I could charge more for the book) they are divided into two sections. The upper walls (New World) are another 600 meters further up the valley on the Little Si Trail.

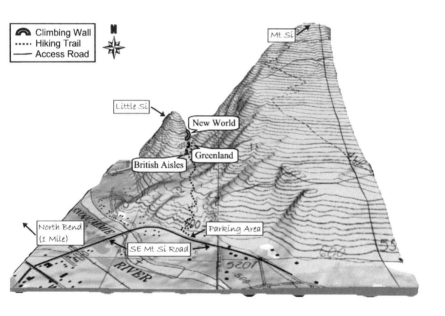

Reach for your dreams and they will reach for you.
- Hana Rose Zadra

Area Summary

Number of Walls	8
Number of Routes	112
Hiking Time	20 minutes to closest wall (Black Stone – .7 mile) 30 minutes to furthest wall (Micro World – .9 mile)
Elevation Gain	390 feet to closest wall (Blackstone) 610 feet to furthest wall (Micro World)
Most Popular Wall	World Wall I

Wall Summary

Wall Name	Height (Meters)	Number of Routes	Hiking Time (Minutes)	Top Rope
Black Stone	30	6	20	No
Repo I	8	5	20	Yes
Repo II	15	7	20	Yes
A.W.O.L	20	8	20	No
Midland	25	4	25	No
Woods	30	20	25	No
World Wall I	45	64	30	No
Micro World	8	4	30	Yes

Wall Difficulty

The following 3D chart shows you the number of routes at a given difficulty rating for each wall. For example, if you were looking to climb 5.5-5.6 level routes, then Blackstone and Repo I are the places to visit. *Note: World Wall I has 58 routes from 5.11b – 5.14b.*

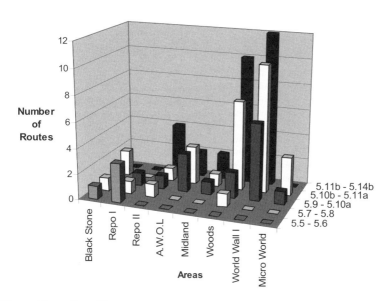

Elevation Profile

This impressive chart says, "trail steep at beginning, then gradual."

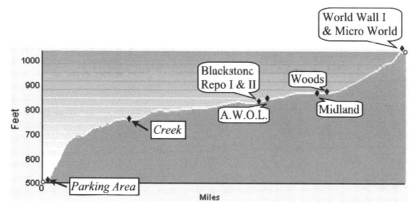

15

The Little Si Climbing Area is 29.53 miles east of Seattle. If you're coming from Seattle, take a left at the top of Exit 32 off Interstate 90 and head north over the freeway on 436th Avenue SE.

Continue driving north on 436th Avenue SE .46 mile. Turn left at the stop sign on SE North Bend Way. Continue for .3 mile and turn right onto SE Mt. Si Road. Drive .37 mile on SE Mt. Si Road. The paved Little Si parking area is on the left side of the road.

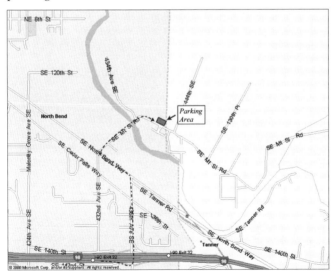

The following map shows the basic layout of the climbing area. The parking area starts from the river basin and gradually climbs the narrow valley between Little Si Mountain and Big Si Mountain through a heavily wooded area. It's .7 mile (20-minute hike) from the parking area to the first climbing walls and .9 mile (30-minute hike) to the furthest walls.

The parking area and trail are new as of August 2002. The State says the reason for the new parking lot and trail was to mitigate the environmental impact to the area and to reduce the foot traffic by the houses on 424th SE Street. Another, and somewhat more believable reason, is a lot of hikers filed complaints because the home owners would let their nasty dogs loose to bite climbers on the butt when they hiked down 434th street from the old parking lot.

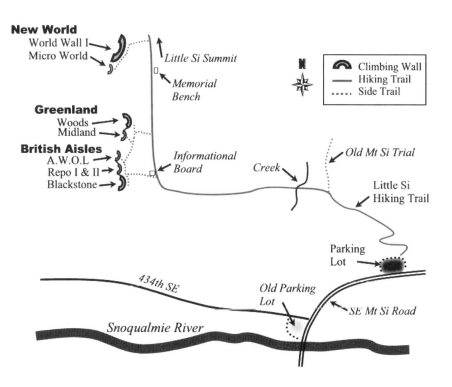

The parking lot serves two purposes. The primary purpose is for people who are hoping to find the summit of the Little Si Mountain. The secondary, but more important, is for people who are hoping to experience the vertical fear and excitement of crawling walls.

The lot has 30½ spacious parking spots, paved, nicely landscaped, easy access, a fresh new toilet, and you don't have to pay to park. Really. The reason is because the Little Si area is part of the Department of Resources conservational area, and not the destitute State Park system.

During the week days you can usually find a space to put your wheels. If the lot is full, drive back up the road 100 meters to the old parking area on the right (west), next to the bridge. The old parking area should be available until the county begins construction on the new bridge in the spring of 2006.

If the old parking lot is full, which will happen on sunny weekends, then drive back across the bridge and park on the shoulder of the road. Note: You may have to throw yourself from the bridge if two large trucks happen to drive across it when you're trying to cross.

Parking Area

SE Mt Si Road

To get to the climbing walls, follow the Little Si hiking trail from the northeast corner (next to the toilet) of the parking lot up the side of the ridge on a series of short switchbacks.

The climbing area is about halfway between the parking lot and the summit of Little Si or .7 mile (20-minute hike). The trail to the summit of Little Si is 1.35 miles or about 45 minutes of enjoyable hiking time.

> *Time is:*
> *Too slow for those who wait,*
> *Too swift for those who fear,*
> *Too long for those who grieve,*
> *Too short for those who rejoice,*
> *But for those who love, time is not.*
> *- Henry Van Dyke*

19

After hiking 10 minutes (.4 miles) up the switch backs from the parking lot, the trail flattens out and forks left (Little Si summit) and right (old Mt Si trail).

Continue on the Little Si trail for another 10 minutes (.3 miles) to an informational board. This marks the beginning of the climbing area.

Note: *Trail improvements are planned for 2004 so the middle section of the hiking trail (top picture above) may be changed. Check http://www.northbendrock.com/bookupdates for current information.*

British Aisles is the first of three climbing areas you'll reach from the parking lot. It has the most beginning level (5.5-5.8) routes. It also catches the most sun of the three areas which makes it one of the more popular places to climb. It has four closely spaced walls: Blackstone, Repo I, Repo II, and A.W.O.L.

At 25 meters high, Blackstone is the largest of the walls in British Aisles. It has five nice sport routes on a juggy, near vertical, face.

Repo I and II are two eight-meter high pillars just to the right of Blackstone in the center of British Aisles. These are the first places that were climbed back in the early 1950's. Really. They are the best place for beginning sport and gear climbing because you can top rope most of the routes.

A.W.O.L is the last of the three crags in British Aisles. It's a big blocky bugger with several pleasant gear routes. In fact, it's the best place to go if you're carrying a nice rack.

British Aisles

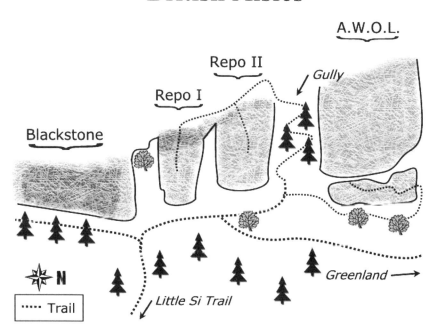

Hike up the Little Si trial 20 minutes (.7 mile) and take the side trail to the left of the bulletin board. Follow this side trail 5 meters up a gradual incline to the walls.

> *Life's tragedy is when we get old too soon and wise too late.*
>
> *   - Benjamin Franklin*

The first wall in the British Aisles group, Blackstone, is, as you may have cleverly guessed, black. The actual rock isn't black. It's the color of the lichen (ascomycetes) which covers most of it. It's a good intermediate wall (5.10's) with a nice beginning 5.8 lead route on the right corner. The wall is 30 meters high, so a 60-meter rope can save you some embarrassment.

Blackstone

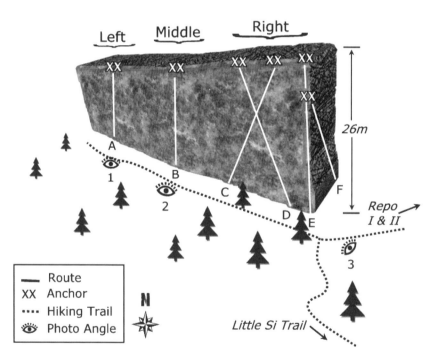

Difficulty	Route	Bolts	Rating	Top Rope	Route Name
5.10a	A	9	★★★	No	The Big Easy ❗ See Beta p. 82

Notes _____

_____

_____

_____

_____

_____

_____

_____

_____

_____

_____

_____

_____

_____

_____

_____

_____

_____

Date _____

5.10c
B

p. 23

Repo I & II →

Difficulty	Route	Bolts	Rating	Top Rope	Route Name
5.10c	B	11	★★★	No	Stepping Stone **!** See Beta p. 84

Notes _____

_____
_____
_____
_____
_____
_____
_____
_____
_____
_____
_____
_____
_____
_____
_____
_____
_____
_____

Date _____

Difficulty	Route	Bolts	Rating	Top Rope	Route Name
5.10b	C	13	★★★	No	BLM-1 ! See Beta p. 83
5.9	D	9	★★★	No	BLM-2 ! See Beta p. 81
5.8	E	8	★★★	No	Human Foot ! See Beta p. 80
5.6	F	4	★★	No	Cranium Teaser p. 80

Danette working the
"Human Foot" – **5.8** (p. 26)

Repo I and II are two small twin pillars 10 meters to the right of Blackstone. Repo I is a great place for beginner climbers because the routes are between 5.5 - 5.9, and they can easily be top roped. Repo II is the larger of the twins, and the routes are more difficult (5.9 – 5.12a).

There is one shared anchor (hangers) at the top of Repo I, and two shared anchors at the top of Repo II. If someone is already using them then you'll have to chuck their rope off when they are not looking or wait until they are done.

To top rope Repo II, follow the trail up the gully on the right. To top rope Repo I, continue across Repo II and then scramble down a couple of large blocks to the hangers at the top of Repo I.

Repo I & II

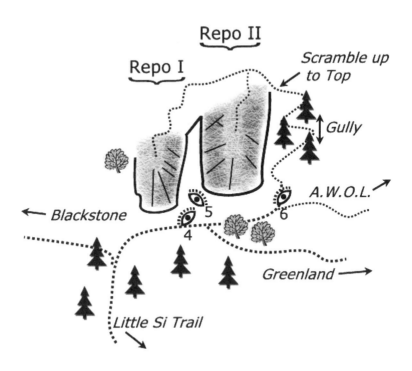

Notes _____

_____

_____

_____

_____

_____

_____

_____

_____

_____

_____

_____

_____

Date _____

Difficulty	Route	Bolts	Rating	Top Rope	Route Name
5.9	A	0 (Pro to 1")	★★	✓	On Second Thought p. 81
5.6	B	0 (Pro to 2")	★★★	✓	First Things Left p. 80
5.6	C	0 (Pro to 2")	★★	✓	First Things First p. 80
5.7	D	0	★	✓	Next Time Around p. 80
5.5	E	0	★★	✓	Three Legged Dog p. 80

p. 28

Notes _____

_____

_____

_____

_____

_____

_____

_____

_____

_____

_____

_____

_____

_____

_____

Date _____

Difficulty	Route	Bolts	Rating	Top Rope	Route Name
5.12c	A	5	★★	✓	Whynosauras p. 92
5.11c	B	2 (Pro to 2")	★★	✓	Trynosaurus p. 88
5.10b	C	2 (Pro to 2")	★★★	✓	Mambo Jambo p. 83
5.12a	D	4 (Pro to 1")	★★	✓	Little Big Man p. 90

Trail to top
of Repo I & II

5.8
B

5.9
A

A.W.O.L.

Repo I

p. 28

Date _____

Difficulty	Route	Bolts	Rating	Top Rope	Route Name
5.9	A	2 (Pro to 1½")	★★	✓	Repo Man p. 81
5.8	B	0 (Pro to 3")	★★	✓	Fixer Upper p. 80

31

A.W.O.L wall is 20 meters to the right of Repo II just across a small gully. It has mostly intermediate routes (5.10a – 5.11b) that range from 17 meters to 22 meters. There are several sweet cracks on A.W.O.L., so if you like to place your own protection, then this is the place to do it.

A.W.O.L. was one of the first sport climbing walls developed in the area and several hangers move freely. You don't have to clip into them, but given the alternative, you most likely will.

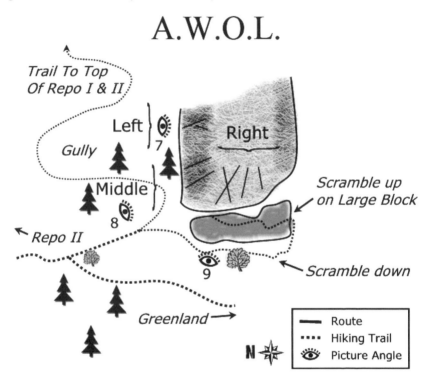

*Notes*_____

_____

_____

_____

_____

_____

_____

_____

_____

_____

_____

_____

_____

_____

_____

_____

_____

*Date*_____

Difficulty	Route	Bolts	Rating	Top Rope	Route Name
5.10c	A	2 (Pro to 4")	★★	No	Collateral Damage p. 84
5.11b	B	7	★★★	No	Situation Room p. 86

Difficulty	Route	Bolts	Rating	Top Rope	Route Name
5.9	C	6	★ ★ ★	No	Kinder, Gentler, Carpet Bombing p. 81
5.11b	D	6	★ ★ ★	No	Little Hitler's p. 86
5.10a	E	0 (Pro to 4")	★ ★	No	You Get What You Deserve p. 82

Notes _____

_____

_____

_____

_____ *Date* _____

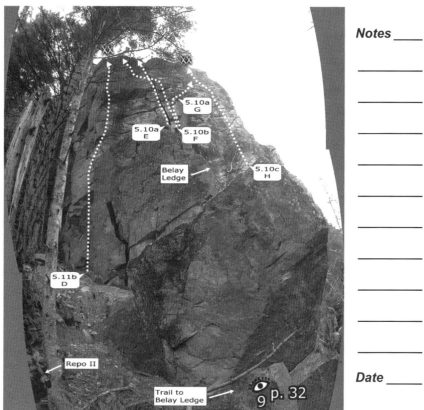

p. 32

Notes ____

____

____

____

____

____

____

____

____

____

____

Date ____

Difficulty	Route	Bolts	Rating	Top Rope	Route Name
5.11b	D	6	★★★	No	Little Hitler's p. 86
5.10a	E	0 (Pro to 4")	★★	No	You Get What You Deserve p. 82
5.10b	F	3 (Pro to 3")	★	No	D.W.I. p. 83
5.10a	G	5	★★	No	Sideswipe p. 82
5.10c	H	6	★★★★	No	Goddess p. 84

Greenland is the middle of the three climbing areas. Its walls are larger than those in British Aisles. It's divided into two sections—Midland and Woods. Midland is the left section, and Woods is to the right section.

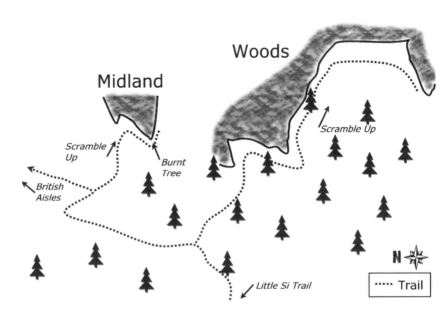

Greenland

Whether you think you can, or think you can not, you are right.
                                        - Henry Ford

To reach the Greenland area, take the first side trail to the left a couple of minutes hike past the bulletin board (p. 20) from the beginning of the climbing area. See the map on p. 17 for more detail.

Trail Marker

To New World

To Greenland

Little Si Trail

Have Faith and pursue the unknown end.
- Oliver Wendell Holmes

The Woods
From the Little Si trail hike 5 meters up a gradual incline to a trail fork. The right trail at the fork leads to The Woods.

Midland
To get to Midland, continue up one switch back past the turn off to The Woods and take the next side trail to the right.

There are two fine arêtes that make Midland. The left arête has a first-class 5.12a route and the right arête has a grand 5.9 route.

The 5.9 arête shares its anchor with a 5.11a combo sport/gear face climb between the two arêtes. If you're a 5.11 wannabe climber or didn't bring any pro, lead the 5.9 route on the arête and then throw the rope over to the 5.11 (which also has a 5.10c option) for a low stress top rope climb.

Midland

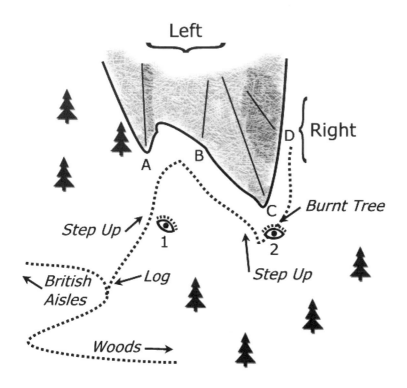

Take time to laugh, it's the music of the soul.
- Anonymous

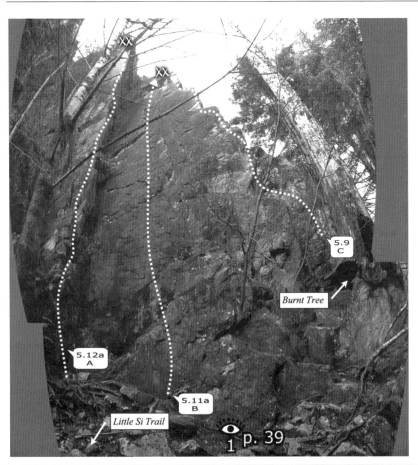

Difficulty	Route	Bolts	Rating	Top Rope	Route Name
5.12a	A	7	★ ★ ★ ★	No	Lay Of The Land **!** See Beta p. 89
5.11a	B	6 (Pro to 1")	★ ★ ★	No	The Nameless Tower p. 85
5.9	C	9	★ ★ ★	No	Sweet And Sticky p. 81

Notes _____

_____ *Date* _____

p. 39

Notes _____

_____
_____
_____
_____
_____
_____
_____
_____
_____
_____
_____
_____
_____

Date _____

Difficulty	Route	Bolts	Rating	Top Rope	Route Name
5.9	C	9	★★★	No	Sweet And Sticky p. 81
5.11b	D	7	★★	No	Violent Phlegms p. 87

All significant battles are waged within the self.
- Sheldon Kopp

Ellie (age 4) Belaying Derik (age 4) on
"First Things First" – 5.6 (p. 29)

As the name suggests, Woods is veiled by trees and is often overlooked by climbers. Like Amazonia in the Mt Washington area at Exit 38, it sees little to no sun given it is enclosed by the trees, but it's a choice place to climb on hot summer days.

At roughly 30 meters, the walls in Woods are a size larger than British Aisles. The routes are mostly in the range of 5.10c – 5.11b. The Woods area is often less crowded than the other areas. This shouldn't be as it has some of the best, well-bolted routes and a couple of fun gear routes.

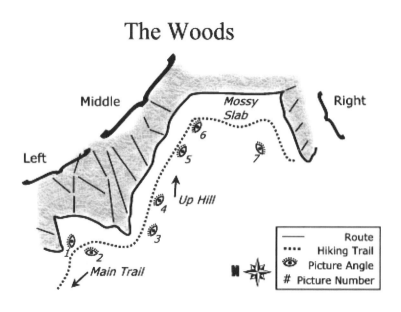

There are two ways to live your life. One is as though nothing is a miracle; the other is as though everything is a miracle.
- Albert Einstein

① p. 43

Difficulty	Route	Bolts	Rating	Top Rope	Route Name
5.12b	A	11	★★★	No	Digitalis p. 91

**Rainy Day Woman Stephanie on
"Rainy Day Women" – 5.12a** (p. 72)

Difficulty	Route	Bolts	Rating	Top Rope	Route Name
5.7	B	2	★★	No	Exhume To Consume p. 80
5.10b	C	5	★★	No	Aeoliatrous Ve Ensomb p. 83
5.11c	D	10	★★	No	Resume To Entomb p. 88
5.12a	E	10	★★	No	Human Glue p. 89
5.10b	F	4	★	No	Incarnated Solvent Abuse p. 83
5.10a	G	5	★★★	No	Streetcleaner p. 82
5.10b	H	6	★★	No	Tablature Of Emotion p. 83
5.11c	I	10	★★★	No	Godflesh p. 88

Notes _____

_____

_____

_____

_____

_____

_____

_____   *Date* _____

3 p. 43

Notes___

Date___

Difficulty	Route	Bolts	Rating	Top Rope	Route Name
5.11b	J	9	★★★	No	Goldrush ! See Beta p. 87
5.11d	K	10	★★★	No	Yo Baby ! See Beta p. 88

Lisa descending to Earth on
"Goddess" – **5.10c** (p. 35)

Notes_____

_____

_____

_____

_____

_____

_____

_____

_____

_____

_____

_____

_____

_____

_____

_____

_____

_____

_____

_____

_____

_____Date_____

Difficulty	Route	Bolts	Rating	Top Rope	Route Name
5.11d	K	10	★★★	No	Yo Baby p. 88
5.12a	L	10	★★	No	Mo Clips p. 90
5.11b	M	6	★★	No	Monkey Madness p. 87

Notes _____

_____

_____

_____

_____

_____

_____

_____

_____

_____

_____

_____

_____

_____

_____

_____

_____

_____

Date _____

Difficulty	Route	Bolts	Rating	Top Rope	Route Name
5.9	N	6 (Pro to 1½")	★★★★	No	Bioclamatic Quandary p. 81
5.12a	O	10	★★	No	State Of Perplexity p. 90

Difficulty	Route	Bolts	Rating	Top Rope	Route Name
5.12b	P	4	★	No	Double Take p. 91

Notes _____

_____ **Date** _____

Difficulty	Route	Bolts	Rating	Top Rope	Route Name
5.10b	Q	0 (Pro to 3")	★★★	No	Only In It For The Money p. 83
5.11a	R	0	★	No	Money For Nothing p. 85
5.10d	S	2	★★	No	Have You Told Your Husband Yet p. 85
5.10c	T	2	★★	No	Garmonbozia p. 84

Notes _____

_____ *Date* _____

New World is comprised of one grand wall, World Wall I (WWI), and one humble wall, Micro World. WWI is the largest rock wall at the Exit 32 area. It's probably fair to say that WWI is the mountain Little Si i.e. it's holding up the summit. Micro World is, ironically, the smallest wall in the area.

World Wall I is an advanced sport climber's dream come true. It is 45 meters high, 70 meters wide, and lightly vertical to heavily overhanging. Of the 58 routes on WWI, 41 are over 5.11b in difficulty.

Micro World is a small chunk of rock with four short routes at the far end of World Wall.

New World

World Wall I

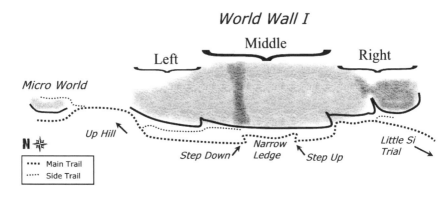

> It's a short trip. While alive, live.
> - Malcolm

To reach the New World area, continue hiking .2 miles (5 minutes) up the Little Si trial past Greenland (or 30 minutes from the parking lot). Take the side trail to the left by the trail marker just past the Doug Hansen memorial bench. The side trail traverses up a short hill to the lower right section of the WWI wall.

To have a great adventure, and survive, requires good judgment. Good judgment comes from experience. Experience, of course, is the result of poor judgment.

-Geoff Tabin

World Wall I is 45 meters of vertical joy on some of the best rock in the state. It's slightly vertical to heavily overhanging and it offers an amazing variety of routes at all difficulty levels. For example, it has one of the states best 5.9's (Reptiles and Amphetamines) adjacent to one of the states best 5.13's (Chronic).

The belay ledge, also referred to as the launch ledge, starts on the lower right section of the wall and traverses up and across the wall via a narrow rock ledge. The ledge is 15 meters above the ground. It's usually not a problem for most climbers, but add a busy weekend, a few nervous beginning climbers, and a loose dog, and you've got potential for injury. Needless to say, be careful when scrambling down the narrow section of the ledge in the middle of the wall, and scrambling up the ledge at the left section of the wall.

World Wall I

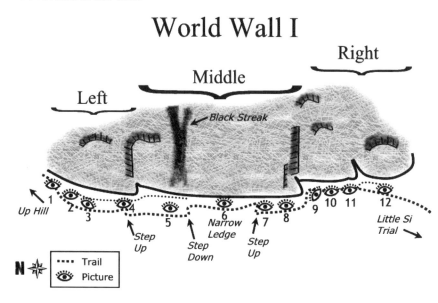

Difficulty	Route	Bolts	Rating	Top Rope	Route Name
5.11b	A	4	★★	No	BLM-3 p. 87
5.10a	B	6	★★	No	BLM-4 p. 82
5.10c	C	8	★★★	No	BLM-5 p. 84

Notes _____

_____

_____

_____

_____

_____ ***Date*** _____

Difficulty	Route	Bolts	Rating	Top Rope	Route Name
5.10c	C	8	★★★	No	BLM-5 p. 84
5.10d	D	10	★★★★	No	BLM-6 p. 85
5.12b	E	9	★★	No	Dairy Freeze p. 91

Notes _____

_____

_____

_____ *Date* _____

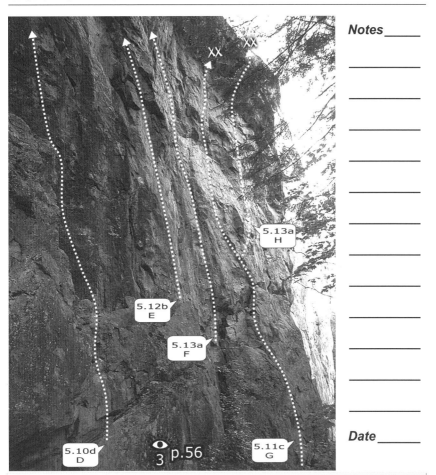

p.56

Notes ____

Date ____

Difficulty	Route	Bolts	Rating	Top Rope	Route Name
5.10d	D	10	★★★★	No	BLM-6 p. 85
5.12b	E	9	★★	No	Dairy Freeze p. 91
5.13a	F	6	★★	No	Black Is All We Feel p. 94
5.11c	G	8	★★★	No	The Bad Guy p. 88
5.13a	H	12	★★	No	Hadley's Roof p. 94

Difficulty	Route	Bolts	Rating	Top Rope	Route Name
5.11b	I	15	★★★★	No	Megatherion p.86
5.12a	J	9	★★★	No	Sweet Tooth p.89

Notes _____

_____ **Date** _____

Josh, love'in the
"Whore Of Babylon" – **5.14b** (p. 64)

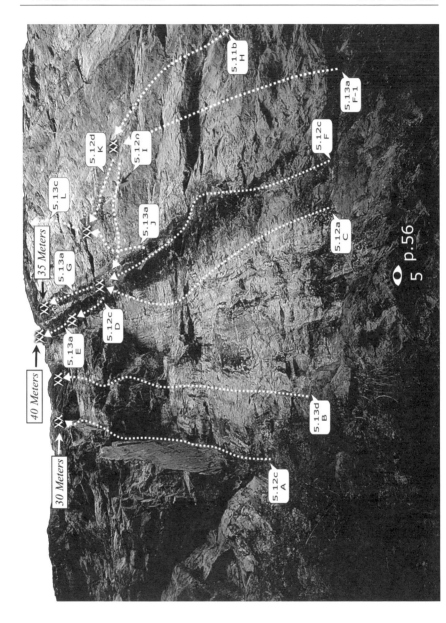

Difficulty	Route	Bolts	Rating	Top Rope	Route Name
5.12c	A	10	★★	No	Slug Lover p. 92
5.13d	B	9	★★★	No	Enigma p. 95
5.12a	C	9	★★★	No	Bust The Move p. 89
5.12c	D	13	★★★	No	Bust The Rhythm p. 92
5.13a	E	19	★★	No	Dreadlock p. 94
5.12c	F	11	★★★★	No	Propaganda p. 92
5.13a	F-1	13	★★	No	Gerbil Killer p. 94
5.13c	G	16	★★★★	No	Black Ice p. 94
5.11b	H	10	★★★	No	Psycho-Wussy p. 86
512.b	I	12	★★	No	Fitness Fanatic p. 91
5.13a	J	9	★★	No	Hard Liner p. 94
5.12d	K	13	★★★★	No	Psychosomatic p. 93
5.13c	L	11	★★	No	Flat Liner p. 94

Notes _____

_____

_____

_____

_____ **Date** _____

Difficulty	Route	Bolts	Rating	Top Rope	Route Name
5.10c	M	6	★★	No	Slaborigine p. 84
5.14b	N	15	★★	No	Whore Of Babylon p. 95
5.11b	O	8	★★★★	No	Aborigine p. 86
5.13d	P	16	★★★★	No	Porn Star p. 95
5.12d	Q	12	★★★★	No	Technorigine p. 92
5.13b	R	11	★★★★	No	Chronic p. 94
5.12d	S	12	★★★★	No	Californicator p. 93
5.14a	W	15	★★★	No	Dr. Evil p. 95

Notes _____

_____

_____

_____

_____

_____

_____

Date

Difficulty	Route	Bolts	Rating	Top Rope	Route Name
5.13b	R	11	★ ★ ★ ★	No	Chronic p. 94
5.12d	S	12	★ ★	No	Californicator p. 93
5.13c	T	13	★ ★	No	Lizard Prince p. 94
5.13c	U	18	★ ★	No	Lizard Queen p. 95
5.13c	V	14	★ ★ ★	No	Extended Illness p. 94
5.14a	W	15	★ ★ ★	No	Dr. Evil p. 95
5.9	X	4	★ ★ ★ ★	No	Reptiles And Amphetamines p. 81

Notes _____

_____

_____

_____

_____

_____ *Date* _____

Never fear that your life may come to a sudden end, rather fear that it may end before it has begun.

-Anonymous

Date _____

Difficulty	Route	Bolts	Rating	Top Rope	Route Name
5.14a	W	15	★★	No	Dr. Evil <div align="right">p. 95</div>
5.9	X	4	★★★★	No	Reptiles And Amphetamines <div align="right">p. 81</div>
5.10b	Y	6	★★★	No	Jug Or Not <div align="right">p. 83</div>
5.13a	Z	16	★★	No	Oval Orifice <div align="right">p. 94</div>

Jeff fighting the fatigue on
"Chronic" – **5.13b** (p. 64)

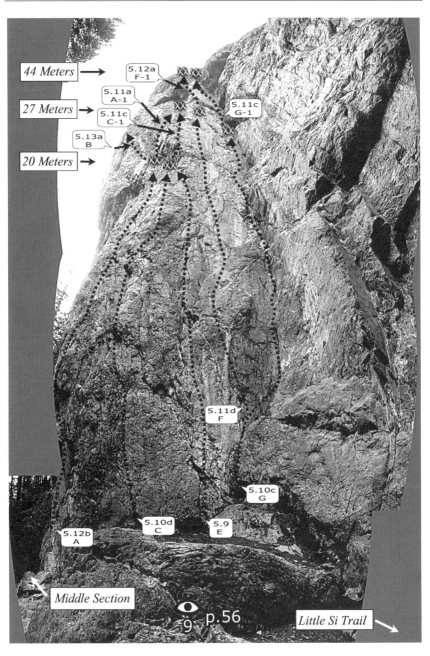

44 Meters →

5.12a
F-1

5.11a
A-1

27 Meters →

5.11c
C-1

5.11c
G-1

5.13a
B

20 Meters →

5.11d
F

5.10c
G

5.10d
C

5.9
E

5.12b
A

Middle Section

9 p.56

Little Si Trail →

Difficulty	Route	Bolts	Rating	Top Rope	Route Name
5.12b	A	6	★	No	Oedipal Complex p. 93
5.11a	A-1	8 (Pro to 2")	★★	No	Sinistral Purpose p. 85
5.13a	B	17	★★	No	Oval Orifice p. 94
5.10d	C	6	★★★	No	Dreaming Of A Life Of Ease (1st Pitch) p. 85
5.11c	C-1	12	★★★	No	Dreaming Of A Life Of Ease (2nd Pitch) p. 88
5.9	E	4	★★★	No	Devil's Advocate p. 81
5.11d	F	9	★★	No	Spent p. 88
5.12a	F-1	18	★	No	Totally Spent p. 90
5.10c	G	10	★★★★	No	Son Of Jesus p. 84
5.11c	G-1	18	★★★★	No	Vudu Guru p. 88

Notes _____

_____

_____

_____

_____

_____

_____

_____

_____ **Date** _____

44 Meters

5.11c
G-1

5.11b
D

35 Meters

5.12d
H-1

5.12b
I-2

5.12d
I-1

5.10c
G

5.12b
H

5.12a
I

5.12b
J

Middle of Wall

p.56
10

Little Si Trail

Difficulty	Route	Bolts	Rating	Top Rope	Route Name
5.11b	D	14	★★	No	Just One Of The Boys p. 86
5.10c	G	10	★★★★	No	Son Of Jesus p. 84
5.11c	G-1	18	★★★★	No	Vudu Guru p. 88
5.12b	H	10	★★★	No	Viagro p. 91
5.12d	H-1	12	★★	No	Viagrophobia p. 93
5.12a	I	12	★★★★	No	Rainy Day Women p. 89
5.12d	I-1	16	★★★	No	Hydrophobia p. 93
5.12b	I-2	17	★★★	No	Deluge p. 91
5.12b	J	11	★★★	No	Hang Out To Dry p. 91

Notes _____

_____

_____

_____

_____

_____

_____

_____ **Date** _____

Difficulty	Route	Bolts	Rating	Top Rope	Route Name
5.12b	J	11	★★★	No	Hang It Out To Dry p. 91
5.9	K	6	★★	No	Opening Act p. 81
5.10c	L	8	★★★	No	Girls In The Gym p. 84
5.13a	M	13	★★	No	Unknown p. 94
5.12c	N	11	★★	No	Judgement Day p. 92
5.12d	O	12	★★	No	Judgement Day Direct p. 93
5.12a	P	12	★★	No	End Of The World p. 90

Notes _____

_____

_____

_____

_____

_____

_____

_____ *Date* _____

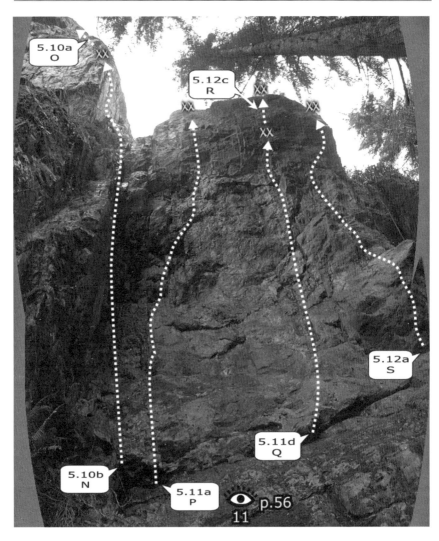

Difficulty	Route	Bolts	Rating	Top Rope	Route Name
5.10b	N	10	★★★	No	BLM-7 p. 83
5.10a	O	10	★★★★	No	BLM-8 **!** See Beta p. 82
5.11a	P	7	★★★	No	Disincarnate p. 85
5.11d	Q	5	★★	No	False Idol p. 88
5.12c	R	6	★★★★	No	Graven Image p. 92
5.12a	S	4	★★★	No	Jealous God p. 89

Notes _____

_____

_____

_____

_____

_____

_____

_____ **Date** _____

Micro World has four short intermediate routes (5.10a – 5.11a) just up the hill from World Wall I. To reach it, continue on the trail past World Wall I up a short hill to a trail fork which leads left and right. Take the left fork and hike for 5 seconds (.00313 mile) to the lower right side of Micro World.

Although Micro World had its first bolts installed a decade ago, it saw few climbers because it was never mentioned in any publications. So why document it now? Two main reasons—it's easy to access, and it has several reasonable boulder problems which can all be top roped. Think of it as a low stress warm up for the big guy next door.

Micro World

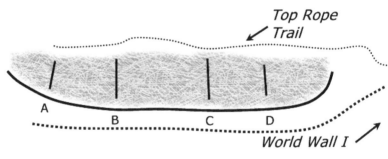

Top Rope Trail

A   B   C   D

World Wall I

N

- Route
- ···· Hiking Trail
- Picture Angle

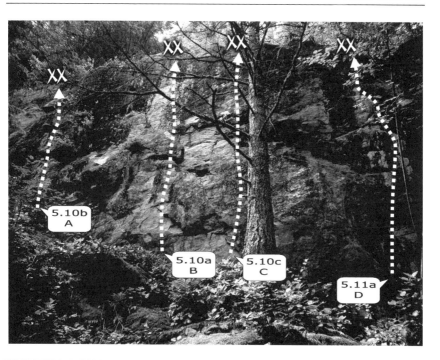

Difficulty	Route	Bolts	Rating	Top Rope	Route Name
5.10b	A	3	★★	✓	Organic Blueberry p. 83
5.10a	B	2	★★	✓	Blackcap Express p. 82
5.10c	C	4	★★	✓	Oregon Grape p. 84
5.11a	D	3	★★	✓	Wild Salmonberry p. 85

Notes _____

_____

_____

_____ **Date** _____

Difficulty	Route Name	Rating	Area	Beta
5.5	Three Legged Dog p. 29	★★	Repo I	Given the big block steps on this route I image a three legged dog wouldn't have much trouble soloing it. FA: Unknown
5.6	First Things Left p. 29	★★★	Repo I	Belay someone on this route and you'll be asking yourself "what are they doing on that arête?" –Drew Fletcher FA: Unknown
	First Things First p. 29	★★	Repo I	What is a route called when it has stairs? Like this one? –Kendal Stever FA: Unknown
	Cranium Teaser p. 26	★★	Blackstone	Scramble up the gully then up the side to the Human Foot anchor. Can continue on to top of wall on Human Foot. Gully can be slippery when wet. Rappel to start of Human Foot. FA: Leland Windham (solo) 12/92
5.7	Exhume To Consume p. 46	★★	Woods	A mini arête, gear crack, corner or face climb, your choice. Miss the second clip and you'll bounce and no, there isn't a giant bird that lives above the roof. FA: Leland Windham
	Next Time Around p. 29	★	Repo I	For a 5.7 route this is pretty balancy and crimpy, not many places for the biceps to save you on it. –Drew Fletcher FA: Unknown
5.8	Human Foot p. 26	★★★	Blackstone	**! Need a 60 meter rope past first anchors for lower.** Feels a bit tougher than 5.8 given it never lets up. You can set a top rope by leading the 5.6 route "Cranium Teaser" to the right. –Kendal Stever FA: Leland Windham (solo) 12/92
	Fixer Upper p. 31	★★	Repo II	Starts up the crack to a ledge on gear and then finishes on the face with a couple of bolts. Good first gear lead. FA: Leland Windham

Route Listing

Difficulty	Route Name	Rating	Area	Beta
5.9	Reptiles And Amphetamines p. 66	★ ★ ★ ★	World Wall I	Step up on the ledge just past the red graffiti circle and follow the bottomless jug ladder up and right to the anchor. FA: Bryan Burdo, Pete Doorish
	Bioclamatic Quandary p. 51	★ ★ ★ ★	Woods	A great route if you're a beginner looking to test some of your gear. It has it all in fine arrangement i.e. big holds to deluxe crack to thin face. FA: Leland Windham
	Sweet And Sticky p. 40	★ ★ ★	Midland	At the final move to the chains keep looking for the jug, it's there, and try not to use the foothold that looks suspiciously like a bolt and hanger. –Drew Fletcher FA: Bryan Burdo, Pete Doorish
	Devil's Advocate p. 70	★ ★ ★	World Wall I	Start on the right near the corner jump into the crack. Many beached whales have been spotted at the anchors. FA: Bryan Burdo, Pete Doorish
	Kinder, Gentler Carpet Bombing p. 34	★ ★ ★	A.W.O.L.	Feeling natural? Do it with gear. Feeling unnatural? Use the bolts. Tree wedgie start on the left or easier step start on the right. FA: Bryan Burdo, Pete Doorish
	BLM-2 p. 26	★ ★ ★	Blackstone	**! Need a 60 meter rope** Look for the most obstacles on the wall and that's the route i.e. under the vertically challenged tree and into the bush. FA: Bryan Burdo
	Opening Act p. 74	★ ★	World Wall I	A pleasant climb, even though it ends in the middle. –Matt Kerns FA: Matt Kerns, Mike Massey
	Repo Man p. 31	★ ★	Repo II	Crack just right of the arête. Nice route for first time gear leads. FA: Unknown
	On Second Thought p. 29	★ ★	Repo I	A popular route primarily because the hiking trail leads directly to it. FA: Unknown 8/51?

Difficulty	Route Name	Rating	Area	Beta
5.10a	BLM-4 p. 76	★ ★ ★ ★	World Wall I	**! If you use a single rope then** stay right on the rappel to reach the first chains or use a double rope to rap to the ground. FA: Bryan Burdo
	The Big Easy p. 24	★ ★ ★	Blackstone	**! Need a 60 meter rope** One of the favorites on the wall. A nice consistent and well behaved 10a. FA: Aaron Houseknecht
	BLM-4 p. 57	★ ★	World Wall I	Far left route on World Wall I. Veer right past the first bolt for the 5.10a then lie back and enjoy the finish. FA: Bryan Burdo
	Streetcleaner p. 46	★ ★ ★	Woods	A dirty job but someone has to do it. Best if done during the day. FA: Leland Windham
	Sideswipe p. 35	★ ★	A.W.O.L.	Start just right of the crack and veer right onto Goddess midway up the face. FA: Bryan Burdo, Pete Doorish
	You Get What You Deserve p. 35	★ ★	A.W.O.L.	Follow the crack up the face to a ledge and veer left to finish on Little Hitler's with a couple of bolts or lower down. FA: Bryan Burdo, Pete Doorish
	Blackcap Express p. 79	★ ★	Micro World	Jug Jug Crimp Jug Jug FA: Leland Windham 3/93

Difficulty	Route Name	Rating	Area	Beta
5.10b	Mambo Jambo p. 30	★ ★ ★	Repo II	Saunter up the flake at the bottom and then veer right to the crack. Don't bother trying to get the rock out. FA: Unknown
	Jug Or Not p. 68	★ ★ ★	World Wall I	Start with a wedgie, then jump into the corner, up, shuffle right, then straight to the chains. Can be top roped from Reptile chains. FA: Bryan Burdo, Leland Windham
	Only In It For The Money p. 53	★ ★ ★	Woods	A Jamm'in good route made even better given it was retro clean in 8/02 by Dave Wolf. FA: Brian Izdepski, Scott Presho
	BLM-1 p. 26	★ ★ ★	Blackstone	**! Need 60 meter rope.** Pull the hump and dance up on big everything to meet Mr. sloper at the chains. 5.9 route crosses it at 6th bolt. FA: Bryan Burdo
	BLM-7 p. 76	★ ★ ★	World Wall I	Starts in the corner to the left of "Disincarnate". Follow the seam up and then dance left to the first chains. FA: Bryan Burdo, Leland Windham
	Aeoliatrous Ve Ensomb p. 46	★ ★	Woods	feminine sens figur mais joli. FA: Leland Windham
	Tablature Of Emotion p. 46	★ ★	Woods	Turn left midway up "Streetcleaner" to finish on "Aeoliatrous Ve Ensomb". FA: Leland Windham
	Organic Blueberry p. 79	★ ★	Microworld	Jug Jug Crimp Jug. FA: Leland Windham 3/93
	Incarnated Solvent Abuse p. 46	★	Woods	Hiking boots would probably work better than climbing shoes for this route. Need to drag a rope or rap back to "Godflesh Chains". FA: Leland Windham
	D.W.I. p. 35	★	A.W.O.L.	Start just right of the crack and swerve left midway up the face. Finish on Little Hitler's anchors. FA: Bryan Burdo, Pete Doorish

Difficulty	Route Name	Rating	Area	Beta
5.10c	Son Of Jesus p. 70	★★★★	World Wall I	Ascend and you shall receive an angelic gift. FA: Bryan Burdo, Andy Cairns
	Goddess p. 35	★★★★	A.W.O.L.	A divine route. Climb it and you will be enlightened. FA: Bryan Burdo, Pete Doorish
	Girls In The Gym p. 74	★★★	World Wall I	Like girls in the gym, this route will get the blood moving, albeit to different areas of the body. FA: Matt Kerns, Mike Massey
	Stepping Stone p. 25	★★★	Blackstone	True to it's name... except for the lefty crux mid way up the route. FA: John Heiman, Aaron Houseknecht
	BLM-5 p. 57	★★★	World Wall I	An amusing pedestal flake start followed by a series of crimper & jug combos. When you can't find the chains look right. FA: Bryan Burdo
	Collateral Damage p. 33	★★	Repo II	A couple of bolts launch you into some grande cracks. FA: Bryan Burdo, Pete Doorish
	Slaborigine p. 64	★★	World Wall I	Starts just left of the tree/block with one hanger to put you on the upper ledge. Follow the crack up and right to "Aborigine". If you like your skin then it's best not to fall. FA: Bryan Burdo, Pete Doorish, Leland Windham
	Garmonbozia p. 53	★★	Woods	New climbing shoes and faith in the feet will are a bonus on this wicked rock texture. FA: Leland Windham
	Oregon Grape p. 79	★★	Microworld	Jug Jug Crimp Crimp Jug Jug FA: Leland Windham

Difficulty	Route Name	Rating	Area	Beta
5.10d	BLM-6 p. 58	★ ★ ★ ★	World Wall I	Got Balance? You'll need it to reach the chains on this, get close, route. FA: Bryan Burdo
	Dreaming Of A Life Of Ease (1ˢᵗ Pitch) p. 70	★ ★ ★	World Wall I	A route with Ease, made more enjoyable given the recent addition of several comfort bolts. FA: John Dowell, Rich Heisler
	Have You Told Your Husband Yet p. 53	★ ★	Woods	Doesn't look like a 10d but those holds aren't as good as they look either. FA: Charles Buell
5.11a	Disincarnate p. 76	★ ★ ★	World Wall I	If you're an overhung kind of climber then this route will keep you pumped until the last crimp move to the chains. FA: Leland Windham
	The Nameless Tower p. 40	★ ★ ★	Midland	A Sport, Gear, Sport combo route. At the mini roof veer left for 5.10b or straight up and over for the 5.11a. Shares anchor with Sweet & Sticky. FA: Dave Tower
	Wild Salmonberry p. 79	★ ★	Microworld	Jug Jug Pinch Crimp Jug FA: Leland Windham 3/93
	Sinistral Purpose p. 70	★ ★	World Wall I	A Sport Gear sandwich. FA: Bryan Burdo
	Money For Nothing p. 53	★	Woods	Top rope only by climbing the routes on either side. FA: Bryan Burdo, Pete Doorish

Difficulty	Route Name	Rating	Area	Beta
5.11b	Megatherion p. 60	★ ★ ★ ★	World Wall I	A little halcyon attitude, followed by prestidigitation, peregrination, and interdigitate will get you to the top. Savor the "Horn Of Plenty". You'll need a 60 if you continue to the second set of chains. FA: Leland Windham, Bryan Burdo
	Aborigine p. 64	★ ★ ★ ★	World Wall I	Short climbers climb, tall climbers reach. One of the more popular routes on the wall. FA: Bryan Burdo, Leland Windham
	Psycho-Wussy p. 62	★ ★ ★	World Wall I	For those climbers who want to climb Psychosomatic but can't. FA: Bryan Burdo
	Little Hitler's p. 34	★ ★ ★	A.W.O.L.	An entertaining route to the 4th bolt then do the mossy mosey up to the chains. FA: Bryan Burdo, Leland Windham
	Situation Room p. 33	★ ★ ★	A.W.O.L.	You might want to put on a leather glove before you dyno to the jug at the crux. FA: Bryan Burdo, Pete Doorish
	Just One Of The Boys p. 72	★ ★	World Wall I	FA: Bryan Burdo, Pete Doorish, Leland Windham

Route Listing

Difficulty	Route Name	Rating	Area	Beta
5.11b	Gold Rush p. 48	★ ★ ★	Woods	**! The chains are at 27 meters** so a 60 can save you a down climb from the block. Scramble up the block and throw yourself onto the face. Face, arête, face arête. Repeat until at chains. FA: John Heiman, Aaron Houseknecht
	Violent Phlegms p. 41	★ ★	Midland	You'll touch most of the rock on the face by the time you reach the chains on this one. Fun left to right finger plank past the third bolt. FA: Dave Haavik, Aaron Houseknecht
	BLM-3 p. 57	★ ★	World Wall I	The last route on the far left side of World Wall I. Take the left off-ramp past the first bolt to a thin face and meet Mr. Crimper & Mrs. Gaston. FA: Bryan Burdo
	Monkey Madness p. 50	★ ★	Woods	Start up the Monkey bar like holds to a lean face and then finish on more Monkey bars. FA: John Heiman

Difficulty	Route Name	Rating	Area	Beta
5.11c	Vudu Guru p. 70	★ ★ ★ ★	World Wall I	**! Chains are at 40 meters** so drag a rope or rappel to the chains at the second pitch of "Dreaming Of A Life Of Ease" and then to the ledge. Continue past "Son Of Jesus" up a supernatural corner. FA: Bryan Burdo, Pete Doorish
	Godflesh p. 46	★ ★ ★	Woods	Cruise up "Streetcleaner" and then feel the "Flesh" burn on a series of "God" like holds. Use long slings on lower section. FA: Leland Windham
	The Bad Guy p. 59	★ ★ ★	World Wall I	… with big biceps enjoys this route, even through the left dance step at the chains. FA: John Heiman
	Dreaming Of A Life Of Ease (2nd Pitch) p. 70	★ ★ ★	World Wall I	Continue the Dream up and around the right edge. You can lower to the ground with a 60 meter rope. FA: John Dowell, Rich Heisler
	Resume To Entomb p. 46	★ ★	Woods	Warm up on "Exhume To Entomb" and then take the two bolt left hand off ramp onto "Digitalis". FA: Leland Windham
	Trynosaurus p. 30	★ ★	Repo II	Don't be afraid to jump on the Trynosaurus. FA: Craig Hadley
5.11d	Yo Baby p. 48	★ ★ ★	Woods	**! Need a 60 meter rope** Yo Baby will please you, if you treat her with a little respect. FA: Bryan Burdo, Aaron Houseknecht
	False Idol p. 76	★ ★	World Wall I	FA: Bryan Burdo
	Spent p. 70	★ ★	World Wall I	This route will leave you spent if your thin face skills or shoes aren't honed. FA: Mike Massey, Matt Kerns

Difficulty	Route Name	Rating	Area	Beta
5.12a	Rainy Day Women p. 72	★★★★	World Wall I	First crux comes early just past the second bolt on a crimped balance move. Take advantage of the ultimate no hands rest; you'll need it for the last crux muscle move at the bulge two bolts short of your goal. FA: Bryan Burdo, Leland Windham
	Lay Of The Land p. 40	★★★★	Midland	**! The first bolt is run out.** Route crescendos up a sharp arête; 5.7->5.10->5.11->5.12. – Jesse Arneson FA: Bryan Burdo, Pete Doorish, Greg White
	Jealous God p. 76	★★★	World Wall I	FA: Bryan Burdo, Leland Windham
	Sweet Tooth p. 60	★★★	World Wall I	It's good to be tall. FA: John Heiman, Keith Wentz
	Bust The Move p. 62	★★★	World Wall I	FA: John Heiman, Keith Wentz
	Human Glue p. 46	★★	Woods	Wrap your legs over your head? Then this route will be easy for you. Don't go deep on the left hand jug just past the lip (sharp edge) or you'll wish you had some human glue to repair your hand. FA: Leland Windham

Route Listing   *Appendix A*

Difficulty	Route Name	Rating	Area	Beta
5.12a	State Of Perplexity p. 51	★★	Woods	FA: Leland Windham
	End Of The World p. 74	★★	World Wall I	Fun, steep, and gymnastic. Crux comes as you head up the arête with a few heel hooks and some great crimps in and outside of the arête. –Blake Lewis FA: Mike Massey, Matt Kerns
	Mo Clips p. 50	★★	Woods	Skip the Monkey bar Madness start and get Mo satisfaction on some crimpy face climbing Clips. FA: John Heiman
	Little Big Man p. 30	★★	Repo II	2 bolts at bottom jump start you to a short thin crack. FA: Bryan Burdo, Pete Doorish
	Totally Spent p. 70	★	World Wall I	Continuation of "Spent" that will leave you thinking it's aptly named. Chains are 43 meters so use your 90 meter rope. FA: Mike Massey

Difficulty	Route Name	Rating	Area	Beta
5.12b	Hang It Out To Dry p. 74	★ ★ ★	World Wall I	Crux is second bolt from the anchor – miss it and you'll be Hanging Out To Dry. –Matt Kerns FA: Matt Kerns, Mike Massey
	Deluge p. 72	★ ★ ★	World Wall I	FA: Bryan Burdo
	Digitalis p. 44	★ ★ ★	Woods	Miss the clip on the second bolt and you'll eat dirt. Optional 11- start via "Resume To Entomb". Needs a good scrub'in. FA: Dave Tower
	Viagro p. 72	★ ★ ★	World Wall I	Optional 11d left detour before anchors for finish on "Son Of Jesus". FA: Matt Kerns, Mike Massey
	Dairy Freeze p. 59	★ ★	World Wall I	Creaming smooth top and bottom with an icy double side pull middle. FA: Leif Johnson
	Fitness Fanatic p. 62	★ ★	World Wall I	FA: Unknown
	Double Take p. 52	★	Woods	Bring your lawnmower. FA: John Heiman

Difficulty	Route Name	Rating	Area	Beta
5.12c	Graven Image p. 76	★★★★	World Wall I	FA: Bryan Burdo, Leland Windham
	Propaganda p. 62	★★★★	World Wall I	Technical and Balancy to an awkward rest. Big moves and monkey climbing above will leave you brainwashed. –Willy Stockman FA: Bryan Burdo
	Technorigine p. 64	★★★★	World Wall I	Start the "Aborigine" extension with a tricky boulder problem and fight the pump on jugs to anchors. Climb above the anchors to clip. 12c until you bag it. Then you'll tell your friends 12b. –Jeff Hamblin FA: Bryan Burdo
	Bust The Rhythm p. 62	★★★	World Wall I	FA: John Heiman
	Judgement Day p. 74	★★	World Wall I	FA: Dave Moroles, Mike Massey
	Slug Lover p. 62	★★	World Wall I	FA: John Heiman
	Whynosauras p. 30	★★	Repo II	Scramble up the gully to a belay bolt and then head straight up to a distant first bolt. Hangers at anchors. FA: Charles Buell

5.12d	Psychosomatic (2nd Pitch) p. 62	★★★★	World Wall I	FA: Bryan Burdo
	Californicator p. 64	★★★★	World Wall I	Climb the first 6 bolts of Chronic and traverse left. Keep going up and left through 2 more boulder problems separated by decent rests. Skip the last bolt on Redpoint. No way you can fall. Dude, they're jugs! – Jeff Hamblin FA: Leif Johnson
	Hydrophobia p. 72	★★★	World Wall I	FA: Bryan Burdo
	Judgement Day Direct p. 74	★★	World Wall I	FA: Dave Moroles
	Viagrophobia p. 72	★★	World Wall I	FA: Jeff Parmenter
	Oedipal Complex p. 70	★	World Wall I	The reason this route doesn't get climbed much is probably because of its name. *(See Sigmund Fraud psychoanalytic theories for more beta.)* FA: Eric Kubiak, Craig Hadley

Difficulty	Route Name	Rating	Area	Beta
5.13a	Hadley's Roof p. 59	★★	World Wall I	FA: Eric Kubiak, Craig Hadley
	Black Is All We Feel p. 59	★★	World Wall I	FA: Erik Kubiak
	Gerbil Killer p. 62	★★	World Wall I	FA: Chris Allegro
	Dreadlock p. 62	★★	World Wall I	FA: John Heiman
	Hard Liner p. 62	★★	World Wall I	FA: Unknown
	Oval Orifice p. 70	★★	World Wall I	Need two ropes to rap from chains. FA: CP Little & Erik Kubiak
	Unknown p. 74	★★	World Wall I	FA: C. P. Little
5.13b	Chronic p. 66	★★★★	World Wall I	Classic Little Si endurance climbing. –Willy Stockman FA: Bryan Burdo, Erik Kubiak
5.13c	Black Ice p. 62	★★★★	World Wall I	Spectacular bouldering up the black streak. Two slopers stand guard at the anchor, more than willing to send you back to the start. –Willy Stockman FA:
	Extended Illness p. 66	★★★	World Wall I	Click second to last bolt on Chronic then head right. Terrific boulder problem through the roof followed by a good sickening pump. –Willy Stockman FA: Bryan Burdo
	Lizard Prince p. 66	★★	World Wall I	FA: Erik Kubiak
	Flat Liner p. 62	★★	World Wall I	FA: Michael Orr

Difficulty	Route Name	Rating	Area	Beta
5.13d	Porn Star p. 64	★ ★ ★ ★	World Wall I	Gain elevation in a hurry as you fly up the wall. Sustained all the way to the end. If you blow the dynamic in the middle you're going to take a least a 30 footer. –Willy Stockman FA: Michael Orr
	Enigma p. 62	★ ★ ★ ★	World Wall I	A bit run out at the start but if you can climb at this level it won't be an issue. FA: Eric Kubiak
	Lizard Queen p. 66	★ ★	World Wall I	FA: Unknown
5.14a	Dr. Evil p. 66	★ ★ ★	World Wall I	FA: Eric Kubiak
5.14b	Whore Of Babylon p. 64	★ ★	World Wall I	FA: Eric Kubiak

Best Routes

For those of you who wish you could climb more but can't take more time off work because you owe too much, here are the routes you've got to climb before your job kills you.

Difficulty	Route Name	Wall	Page	Stats			
Best Exit 32 Routes							
5.5	Three Legged Dog	Repo I	29	□ Lead	□ Top Rope	□ Redpoint	□ Flash
5.6	First Things Left	Repo I	29	□ Lead	□ Top Rope	□ Redpoint	□ Flash
5.7	Exhume To Consume	Woods	46	□ Lead	□ Top Rope	□ Redpoint	□ Flash
5.8	Human Foot	Black Stone	26	□ Lead	□ Top Rope	□ Redpoint	□ Flash
5.9	Reptiles And Amphetamines	World Wall I	66	□ Lead	□ Top Rope	□ Redpoint	□ Flash
5.9	Bioclamatic Quandary	Woods	51	□ Lead	□ Top Rope	□ Redpoint	□ Flash
5.9	Sweet And Sticky	Midland	40	□ Lead	□ Top Rope	□ Redpoint	□ Flash
5.10a	BLM-8	World Wall I	74	□ Lead	□ Top Rope	□ Redpoint	□ Flash
5.10a	The Big Easy	Black Stone	44	□ Lead	□ Top Rope	□ Redpoint	□ Flash
5.10b	Mambo Jambo	Repo II	30	□ Lead	□ Top Rope	□ Redpoint	□ Flash
5.10b	BLM-1	Black Stone	25	□ Lead	□ Top Rope	□ Redpoint	□ Flash
5.10c	Son Of Jesus	World Wall I	70	□ Lead	□ Top Rope	□ Redpoint	□ Flash
5.10c	Goddess	Woods	35	□ Lead	□ Top Rope	□ Redpoint	□ Flash
5.10d	Dreaming Of A Life Of Ease	World Wall I	70	□ Lead	□ Top Rope	□ Redpoint	□ Flash
5.10d	BLM-6	World Wall I	59	□ Lead	□ Top Rope	□ Redpoint	□ Flash

Best Routes

				Best Exit 32 Routes			
Difficulty	**Route Name**	**Wall**	**Page**			**Stats**	
5.11a	Disincarnate	World Wall I	76	☐ Lead	☐ Top Rope	☐ Redpoint	☐ Flash
5.11b	Megatherion	World Wall I	60	☐ Lead	☐ Top Rope	☐ Redpoint	☐ Flash
5.11b	Aborigine	World Wall I	64	☐ Lead	☐ Top Rope	☐ Redpoint	☐ Flash
5.11c	Godflesh	Woods	46	☐ Lead	☐ Top Rope	☐ Redpoint	☐ Flash
5.11c	Vudu Guru	World Wall I	70	☐ Lead	☐ Top Rope	☐ Redpoint	☐ Flash
5.11d	Yo Baby	Woods	48	☐ Lead	☐ Top Rope	☐ Redpoint	☐ Flash
5.12a	Rainy Day Women	World Wall I	72	☐ Lead	☐ Top Rope	☐ Redpoint	☐ Flash
5.12a	Jealous God	World Wall I	76	☐ Lead	☐ Top Rope	☐ Redpoint	☐ Flash
5.12b	Deluge	World Wall I	72	☐ Lead	☐ Top Rope	☐ Redpoint	☐ Flash
5.12c	Graven Image	World Wall I	76	☐ Lead	☐ Top Rope	☐ Redpoint	☐ Flash
5.12c	Propaganda	World Wall I	62	☐ Lead	☐ Top Rope	☐ Redpoint	☐ Flash
5.12d	Technorigine	World Wall I	64	☐ Lead	☐ Top Rope	☐ Redpoint	☐ Flash
5.12d	Psychosomatic	World Wall I	51	☐ Lead	☐ Top Rope	☐ Redpoint	☐ Flash
5.13a	Hadley's Roof	World Wall I	59	☐ Lead	☐ Top Rope	☐ Redpoint	☐ Flash
5.13b	Chronic	World Wall I	66	☐ Lead	☐ Top Rope	☐ Redpoint	☐ Flash
5.13c	Black Ice	World Wall I	62	☐ Lead	☐ Top Rope	☐ Redpoint	☐ Flash
5.13d	Enigma	World Wall I	62	☐ Lead	☐ Top Rope	☐ Redpoint	☐ Flash
5.13d	Porn Star	World Wall I	64	☐ Lead	☐ Top Rope	☐ Redpoint	☐ Flash

Facilities

Facilities are limited in each of the climbing areas. Exit 32 has a permanent toilet at the parking area but nothing at the climbing area.

Since North Bend is so close, most out-of-town climbers crash at one of the inexpensive North Bend motels which are only a couple of miles from the climbing parking area. For more information on hotels and restaurants in the area check http://www.snovalley.org.

Camping

Camping in the Snoqualmie valley is really hit-or-miss. If it's a week day and not close to a holiday, then you can probably find a relatively quiet camp spot. If it's a warm and sunny holiday weekend, then you'll most likely be spending the night in your car. The campgrounds are normally only open from early May to mid October.

The closest full service privately owned camping area (showers, phone, power, cable TV hookup, etc.) to the town of North Bend is Snoqualmie River Camping and RV Park. It is 16.4 miles west of the climbing area just outside the town of Fall City. It is located next to the Snoqualmie River and not one, but two, golf courses next to it. They charge around $20 per night for a tent but for only $8 you can use the facilities (shower, phone, etc.) during the day. Note: 25 people per vehicle limit.

The closest state owned camping area (water, toilets, but no showers) is Tinkham campground. It is 10 miles further east on Interstate 90 at Exit 42. To reach it, take the east bound Exit 42 and turn right at the top of the off-ramp and then left onto a dirt road. Follow the dirt road for 1.5 miles and the campground turnoff will be on your left. There is a $7 per day camping fee. It's open from May 16th to Sept 15th. For more information on camping in the area see http://www.parks.wa.gov.

Exit 32 is usually too cold and wet to climb in the winter months between November and March, but from May to September it's superb. Sunny spring days and comfortable summer temperatures make it one of the best places to climb in the state.

The Northwest has a weather pattern that is uniquely different from the rest of the United States in that temperatures and rainfall can vary remarkably in a short distance. These differences are due primarily to the varied topography in the region; so even though it may be sunny in Seattle it might be raining at the climbing area.

As you can tell from the graph below the monthly temperature (and sunshine) increase steadily in the spring and summer averaging a comfortable 75 degrees Fahrenheit in August.

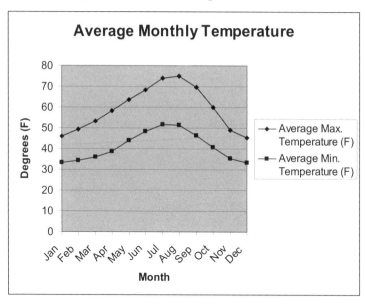

Contrary to popular opinion, the Pacific Northwest does not get more rainfall then the Amazon basin in South America. Seattle receives less rainfall per year than Atlanta, Miami, or Boston. It will probably rain only if you're in town for the weekend and you're really looking forward to some climbing.

The freezing level in the area is around 2,500 feet in the winter and the summit of Little Si Mountain, which is the top of the climbing area, is 1,576 feet. It rarely sees snow in the winter. Some people say the Indian word "Snoqualmie" means "wind tunnel" and they might be right. You can get blow-off routes at Exit 38, but Exit 32 is nicely sheltered from the rude Snoqualmie valley winds by Mt Si.

The graph below shows the average monthly rainfall for the Seattle area in a one year period. Although the graph gives you a good idea of what months get the most rain, it's actually worse than it looks. What I mean is the North Bend area will receive about 15% more rain than the Seattle area during the winter because North Bend is at the base of the Cascade Mountains.

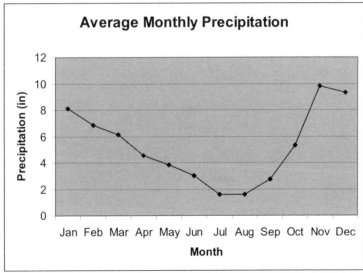

The data points in the graph above were provided by the Western Regional Climate Center. The reporting period is from 1/ 1/1931 to 12/31/2000.

Climbing Area Seasons

The best months to climb at Exit 32 are May through September. Although you can climb there during the winter, given a few days of warm and dry weather, most of the walls are too wet and cold. All the climbing walls at Exit 32 face east and it should be sunny all morning long, but Mt Si blocks all but a few moments of sun during the day.

Being sandwiched in-between Little Si Mountain and Big Si Mountain has its advantages. It has an enjoyable alpine feel, and it is sheltered from the strong Snoqualmie valley winds that can be irritating.

Here's a quick summary for each of the walls in the areas:

- Repo I and II and World Wall I receive the most sun and warmth during the morning and early afternoon.

- In the early afternoon, the sun disappears from the narrow valley.

- The Woods are occluded by wood (go figure) and see little to no direct sun during the summer or winter.

- The upper section of World Wall I is above the trees in the valley and catches the most all around sun in the morning and is shaded and pleasantly cool in the afternoon and evening.

- World Wall I wall stays the driest during the winter given its overhung 10 – 15 meters.

- The routes "Dr. Evil" and "Reptiles & Amphetamines" on World Wall I are great climbs, even during a nasty rain storm.

Area climbing rules

All of the routes at the Exit 32 climbing area are located on public lands and are governed by a set of rules and regulations. To review the current Washington State Conservation Area rules, check the informational sheet on the bulletin boards at the climbing areas. In general, try your best to follow these basic guidelines:

- **ASPIRE TO CLIMB WITHOUT LEAVING A TRACE,** especially in environmentally sensitive areas like caves. Chalk can have a significant impact on dark and porous rock—don't use it around historic rock art. Pick up litter, and leave trees and plants intact.

- **DISPOSE OF HUMAN WASTE PROPERLY.** Use the toilet at the trailhead whenever possible. If you're at the climbing area and it's unavoidable, dig a "cat hole" at least six inches deep and 200 feet from any water, trails, or the base of climbs. Always pack out toilet paper.

- **USE EXISTING TRAILS.** Cutting switchbacks causes erosion. When walking off-trail, tread lightly. Be aware that "rim ecologies" (the clifftop) are often highly sensitive to disturbance.

- **BE DISCRETE WITH FIXED ANCHORS.** Placement of bolts and fixed anchors is only approved for enhancement of safety on existing routes. Creation of additional routes in the area is currently not allowed.

- **RESPECT THE RULES** and speak up when other climbers don't. The climbing area is part of a State designated conservation area. Climbing here is designated by special permission from the Department of Natural Resources. Please do not abuse it or we could lose it.

- **MAINTAIN A LOW PROFILE.** Leave the boom box and day-glo clothing at home — the less climbers are heard and seen from the Little Si hiking trail, the better.

- **RESPECT PRIVATE PROPERTY.** Be courteous to land owners. Don't hike or climb on the surrounding private property.

- **VOLUNTEER.** Through out the year there are opportunities to help maintain and support the climbing area. Check the bulletin boards at the parking area and climbing area for more information.

- **JOIN THE ACCESS FUND.** To become a member, make a tax-deductible donation of $25. For more information surf to http://www.accessfund.org

Local Area Gyms & Indoor Walls

Everett
Cascade Crags   (425)258-3431   www.cascadecrags.com

Issaquah
Sammamish Club   (425)313-3131   www.sammamishclub.com

Kitsap
Vertical World   (360)373-6676   www.verticalworld.com

Redmond
Vertical World   (425)881-8826   www.verticalworld.com
RAC   (425)883-4449   www.redmondathleticclub.com

Seattle
Stone Gardens   (206)781-9828   www.stonegardens.com
REI   (206) 223-1944   www.rei.com/stores/seattle
Vertical World   (206)283-4497   www.verticalworld.com

Local Area Climbing Supply Stores

Bellevue
Marmot Mountain   (425)453-1515   www.marmotmountain.com

North Bend
Pro Ski Service   (425) 888-6397   www.proguiding.com

Redmond
REI   (425) 882-1158   www.rei.com/stores/redmond

Seattle
The North Face   (206)622-4111   www.northface.com
Feathered Friends   (206)283-4497   www.featheredfriends.com
REI   (425)223-1944   www.rci.com/stores/seattle

Local Climbing Guides and Instructors

(See http://www.northbendrock.com/reference/guides for a current list of
local area climbing guides and instructors.)

If you have found this book helpful or maybe even think it's one of your better rock climbing guides that you've purchased or stolen then it's in large part due to the many people that contributed their time and effort to provide me valuable feedback.

Special thanks to the World Wall climbing family whose contributions regarding the more difficult routes were essential. They include Josh Simoneaux, Willy Stockman, Warren Schuchman, Brian Wilkin, Rudy Ruana, Jeff Hamblin, Ryan Triplett, Marcus Hysert, and Blake Lewis.

Also, I would like to say thanks to Leland Windham and Bryan Burdo for their early technical reviews, Ingrid Deermore for reviewing the book at least a dozen times, Matt Kerns for some critical "just in time" route data. Dave Argento for yet more camera instruction, Steve Greenberg for some detailed reviews and layout suggestions, Lisa Lathe for countless suggestions, belays, and laughter, Gary & Christine Perkowski for no particular reason, Kurt Griffis for not letting the taxi driver throw me out on I-5, Tim O'Brien for things I can't print in this book, Drew Fletcher and Kendall Stever for great beta, belays, beer, but mostly BS, Kelly Heintz and Dave Olson for rewriting the regulations section, and my little girl Ellie for helping me to keep this project in perspective.

There are many supporting organizations which help maintain the climbing area. A few I've had the pleasure of working with include Friends of the Trails, Access Fund, Washington State Department of Natural Resources, and Seattle Mountain Rescue. With their constant support the area will continue to be one of the best in the State.

I would also like to say thanks to the many people who have contributed their time and effort into developing the routes at Little Si. Without their dedication to the sport the Exit 32 climbing area wouldn't exist. They include, Bryan Burdo, Leland Windham, Pete Doorish, Eric Kubiak, Matt Kerns, Dave Moroles, Mike Massey, Aaron Houseknecht, Andy Cairns, Charles Buell, John Dowell, Rich Heisler, Dave Tower, John Heiman, John Dowell, Keith Wentz, Greg White, Leif Johnson, Craig Hadley, Mike Orr, and of course, Unknown.

Last but not least, I would like to thank you, the person who purchased this climbing book, even though you probably had a free copy of the Preview.